(My) PAIN is Beauty

Alya Skye

For David Wayne Lewis

A loving son, brother, friend,
husband, and father.

Your life's (taught)
beauty strengthened me to
fight through my pain.

"A bird's beauty doesn't end
with the color of its wings.
Its beauty continues within
the weathered feathers
by its inner storm.
I am Pretty Bird."

Alya Skye

Table of Contents

Pretty Bird Takes Flight

02
Daddy Help Me Understand

10
Stage Four

11
Street Lights (Man's Life)

12
Daddy's Little Girl

14
Unjust Acts

18
"Give Me Your Soul"

20
Broken Shoulders

22
Consequences of Control

23
Solutions

Into The Storm

26
Pretty Bird

29
Mastermind of Deceit

30
Crystal Waters

33
A Hardened Heart

34
Quiet Canvas

37
Blank Canvas

38
Prima Ballerina

41
Reverie

42
Pretty Storm

45
A Silver Platter and A Golden Spoon

Clear Skies

49
The One Who Keeps Knocking

50
I am Peter

52
"You Can't Have The Soul
You Never Created"

53
Naked Love

56
White Flag

57
I Am Pretty Bird

61

Acknowledgments

65

About the Author

Preface

To speak of my father now in the past tense pains me. When I close my eyes, my mind paints his picture. It is so clear that sometimes I'm fooled into thinking that if I reach out, I'll touch him once more. God blessed me with 19 years of life with him.

He was everything I needed and more than what I could have asked for. He chose to love me every day. These poems summarize my journey. Writing them helped me come to terms with the pain I felt and soothe my time of brokenness. I journeyed through the breaking of my faith.

I walked down tunnels with others who sought to stop me from seeing the light at the end. I opened my heart to hate and shared laughs with Satan. I turned a deaf ear to life's calling and walked away from many talents. But I serve a God who never stopped knocking. I accepted life's pain, and He chose to show me its beauty: Love, my purpose, untapped strength, and a testimony to share. To you, my readers, this is my testimony of how my pain became beauty.

Pretty Bird
Takes Flight

Daddy Help Me Understand

*First poem written and recited
for my father's funeral: 07/03/16*

Dad, I know you're somewhere better now,
In a place where you no longer hurt.
But I can't help but wish you back to me,
In your arms where I was first.

God blessed me
When he handpicked you to be my dad.
But as I woke Wednesday morning
To the words, "he has passed,"
All I could do
Was look up and be mad.

Dad, help me understand this purpose.
Why were you taken from me so soon?
You were my protector, provider,
friend, and inspiration;

You took me as a flower seed
and taught me to bloom.

Daddy, my emotions run high,
As thoughts race by,
And I think of all the plans we made.
That you would come to my
college track meets,

Walk me down the aisle,

Hold my kids in your arms;
All things you now
Won't be able to make.

Daddy, who's supposed to
do those things now?
You're a man who cannot be replaced.
You knew me in every way,
You were my ace.

I know I must continue,
As the girl you raised me to be.
But all things I do now,
Shall be in character
That I won't recognize as me.
Daddy, did you know how
special you were to me?

I can still hear your laughter,
As I think back to all the
conversations we had.
You were one of a kind.
I am blessed to have called you my dad.

Daddy, help me understand.
You always came to my aid,
Even when I was undeserving
of your kindness,
You always stayed.

You took me out on dates,
Where you showed me
How to be treated as a woman.
Taught me to be independent.
Think on my own,
Pray for understanding,
Get up when I fell down,
And never let the enemy see me frown.

Strive for greatness,
I deserved no less.
To always stay calm,
No need for me to stress.

Critiqued me when I was wrong,
You developed me to be strong.
Stand on my own two feet,
Never give in to the heat.

Be a woman with her empire.
Keep the boys at arm's length,
And let them admire.

Stand out from the crowd,
Make your family proud.
Be different,
Be unique,
Don't let anyone change Dominique.
You taught me my worth,
And always put me first.

Taught me to drive my arms,
Lift my legs,
And finish all the way.
Even when I screamed at you,
And threw my towel in,
You cleaned it,

And threw it back my way.
You brought me up in the church.
You taught me in the Word.
You are a man after God's own heart.
I see why He did what He did,
He wanted you to help me have a great start.

Daddy, I'm angry.
I'm hurt.
I'm so confused.
Whose shoulder do I cry on?
Who do I call on?
Now you are gone.

Please, dad come back.
End this terrible nightmare.
Your loss is too much for me to bear.

Daddy, you are the greatest man
I will ever know.
I'm thankful,
I'm blessed,
And overjoyed,

You helped me to grow.

All the words that were said today,
Would never be enough
To portray the man
You were to everyone.

I can go on for a lifetime,
Saying all the things you've
ever done for me.
You did what you did,
Out of love and need.

But daddy help me understand,
Why do I feel so alone?
Family and friends surround me,
But I'm missing the most significant part,
You, my stone.

I know mommy cries,
And Daniel and David
Question why?

Every day I wake up,
How I wish I were still asleep
in the middle of a terrible dream.
I try not to question God,
But these acts were so mean.

Dad, I will miss you so much.
I'm going to miss your texts,

Your calls,
And your voice.
I'm going to miss you screaming
at my practice,
And your presence at my meets;
Your absence feels so unreal.

I'm going to miss your hugs,
Your scent,
And your smile.
You made growing up
All worthwhile.

Daddy help me understand,
Why you?
Why now?
Am I selfish,
For wanting you back now?
My inner battle can be labeled rebellious
As I fight to keep from pushing God away
And putting Him on a shelf in hopes for a brighter day.

I know that the dark days are now,
But light is soon to come.
That I should keep my faith in God,
The Holy Spirit,
And His Son.

I should not lean on my understanding.
But to entrust in Him my everything.

Lift my hands in prayers
And to Him,
I shall sing.

Know there's power in prayer,
And that God has the final say.
That we're put through tests
To determine our faith.

You brought the Lord to this house,
And here the Lord shall stay.
I am angry,
Hurt and sad,
But I will not push the Lord
Out of my way.

You're no longer in pain.
No misery,
Nor trembling of the tongue.
You are with your Creator now,
Back jumping,
As if you were young.

Daddy, I want you to know,
That you did your part.
Now it is my turn,
To finish your great start.

I had 19 beautiful years with you,
For each I am thankful.
You inspired me to follow through,

And for that I am grateful.

I know you fought to stay with us,
And tried hard not to leave this way.
I'm letting you know we'll be okay.
I'll think of you every day.

You left David,
Daniel, and I in excellent arms.
Mom will do her best,
To finish the rest.

I will forever be your prima donna,
Your angel,
And your baby girl.
You now have the best seat
In the stadium.
Now watch me shine in this world.

We love you, dad.

Stage Four

You arrive with no expiration date,
Consuming the Goliath's of giants
Misconfiguring their state.

You aim to cripple and consume,
Stripping loved ones
From families too soon.

Stage four is the body's biggest fear.
Causing pain is your purpose,
Quiet cries fall on deaf ears.

You take with no apology,
Leaving your victims
Eyes raised, asking, "why me?"

Street Lights (Man's Life)

From life's first sight,
You opened your eyes to daylight.

Walking in dreams and steady feet,
Learning of life and its bittersweet.

Falling in love and remaining content,
Pouring into seeds with purposeful intent.

Touching the hearts of those in need,
Finishing your task,
He entrusted you to lead.
A warrior who fought from dusk 'till dawn,
And then you walked home
When the street lights came on.

Daddy's Little Girl

Dad, forgive me.
I know you didn't raise me
To holster anger in my heart.
You taught me to love
And to forgive.
But I cannot hold back this rage
That rests in my soul,
Towards the One who knew well
What He was doing from the start.

Continue your eternal rest in peace.
Cover your ears,
Block out all of the sounds.
Close your eyes,
And Shut them tight.
Do not bear witness to this battle
I am willing to fight.
This anger of mine
May take some time to settle.

I know I've already lost.
I'm no match for Him on my best days.
But His acts towards you
Have equipped me with Hell's fire
That burns knowing He's the reason
We are now separated always.

You were taken too soon from this Earth,
Leaving me alone in this world.
God stripped me of my once held title
Of being daddy's little girl.

Unjust Acts

Fair warning for You,
I do not intend to hold back.

My last prayer,
If You still answer those,
Is that every word I say
Rips through the winds around me.
Breaks through the clouds
And separates the skies.
Rockets throughout all space and time
Until they find You.

Let every word,
Meet You Where You're at.
Come out from behind the gates
Where You reside, And HEAR ME!

Hear my cries.
Hear my pain.
Hear my anger.
Hear my screams.
Watch me break before You,
By the hands You call clean.

Watch me crumble to nothingness
By Your actions.
Watch me bow my head
in despair before You.

Witness Your daughter fall from grace
By the acts in which
You would still call JUST.

How could You let this be?

My father was a praying man!
One who revered You,
And still managed to whisper
Your name amid his pain.
You were lifetimes away
Out of range to hear his cries
But I was steps away,
Making out every mumble
And short breath.
I watched my dad
Shrivel up before me.
Lose his ability to walk and talk.
Some days,
That is all that I can see.
A figure that was weakened
And died weighing less than me.

Yet, You still want me to thank you!?
Set my sights on You above?
Remind me again
Of your kind of LOVE.

I question You now.
Were You seeking to teach me a lesson?

Test me on my faith?
Was the foundation in which I stood
Not enough for You, my Grace?

I asked You to ease up on him.
Prayed to you a million times
Had my head filled with promises
From those who said
Your hand was in it all.

Foolish I was.
I came to realize,
That in fact
Your hands were always there.
But not to heal,
They strangled him

Until his body
Gave up the fight for air.

I now realize
This distant conversation with YOU
Will no longer suffice.
I cannot come to You,
So leave YOUR Throne,
And meet me here.
A death wish
Some would call it
But I see it as necessary.
What more could I lose?

It's time for You to face me.
You owe me at least
That one due.

You were supposed to be a God
Who never makes a mistake.
The One who sees all
And knows best
That scripture is so fake.

You are powerful,
That's a Biblically proven fact.
Look at what You've done to me,
Your greatest UNJUST ACT.

"Give Me Your Soul"

You waited patiently for me
Rested in the shadows,
Watching me fall from grace swiftly
I no longer wanted to walk
By faith I could not see.

In my season of spiritual death,
You don't want my life
Needing a body of breath
As evidence of stealing His child
And addicting her to sin's meth.

You constantly reminded me
Of who it was I lost
Wanting to keep me broken,
You bound my flesh
With men who accost.
Luring me into your debt,
Ensuring I stacked up a bill
Of permanent cost.

So, no turning back now,
I won't.
Better the devil I know
Than the devil I don't.

Extolling yourself on what you stole,
And whispering next,
"Give me your soul."

Broken Shoulders

I believe that life is supposed
to be a challenge
He tests our character,
And breaks all limits.
He's tasked to pinpoint our insecurities,
And expose them.
Make us face our reflection,
So that we may grow to love it.

Life will shake us at our core.
Then sit back
And watch our faith break.
He loves most
When we question Him.
Asking why me?
Why now?
Why again?
Why so much?
Because then,
He's done his job.
And places himself on broken shoulders.

The longer we fight against his Master's will,
The heavier he becomes.
Only by our surrender,
Does he begin to abstain.
The way you view life,
Will determine how you'll carry him.

Consequences of Control

Time waits for no one
Life passes by those who blink slowly
The sun rises and sets,
Uncaring of an unfinished schedule
Death is inevitable,
And is assigned to us with a
predetermined expiration date.

Trying to control what you never created,
Leads to your absence in a
space you were needed,
And ceasing to exist in a season
where you were supposed to thrive.

Solutions

Spend time with those who
remain in heartbeat
Walk quickly to your life's purpose
Seek after the joys of today
than the plans of tomorrow
Love the life you did not earn.

Into The Storm

Pretty Bird

Pretty bird, pretty bird,
Takes flight from her tree.
Wings spread wide,
Gliding through the sky,
Pretty bird flies young and carefree.

Heart full of hope,
And spirit filled with joy.
Pretty bird soars
Into a world of the unknown.

New to its aroma,
Seeking adventure and thrills
But pretty bird is unaware
The risks of flying alone.

She was warned of the world's dangers,
And its grasp on naive minds
But pretty bird is determined
To never just follow the lines.

Independent she is
Strong-willed she stands
Pretty bird believes
Her fate is in her hands.

Seeking love, life's firsts,
New beginnings, and encounters

Pretty bird is voyaging
To find her way,
Little did she know,
There was a storm that awaits.

The air became thicker,
White clouds turned grey
Thunder began to rumble,
And the sun slowly disappeared.
Pretty bird was not ready
To lose control of her steer.

She was tossed and twisted,
Slowly becoming a victim to the winds
She became limp with thoughts
Of never seeing clear skies again
Pretty bird, pretty bird,
No longer flies high and carefree
Surviving her storm,
Has become her new journey.

Mastermind of Deceit

In the morning,
There's an order in which I dress
Cleansing myself of last night's sins
And draping on ironed linen
to cover up my mess.

I crown my head in a curtain of hair,
In an attempt to hide my face
Sliding on my costume jewelry,
Then take out my makeup case.

A sheet of brown I layer on,
To cover the lies I'll tell today
A scarf placed over his imprints,
To block the memory of having my breath taken away.

I blush up my cheeks and gloss my lips,
My mask is now complete
Another day I am to be,
The mastermind of deceit.

Crystal Waters

She dared to see her reflection
Removed the mask to find her face
Staring back so paper-thin
Hypnotized by what she sees,
For time had taken its toll
On what used to be uncovered skin.

He praised her for her beauty
But made sure the world could never see
Raining words that watered her flower,
Opening petals by whispered
winds of "trust me."

She found herself outmatched for
this seasoned mastermind of deceit.

Oh crystal waters,
With thee she shall lay
No longer can she wear
The painted face every day.
Allow your waters to consume her figure
Carry to safety the soul that traveled astray.

The two become one.
A new journey for her has begun.
Maskless, she returns to true form
A smile perches her lips,
As her heart begins to run
Beat by beat; she rises closer to the sun

A Hardened Heart

They ask her why she walks around
With such a hardened heart
Her whispers fall on deaf ears,
She's answered from the start.

She shared her story first,
Of her heart's encounter of "love."
Its wrath grasping her neck,
Promising a return to her Creator above.

She showed what little faith,
And the small hope she had in men
When "good" came to her steps,
He failed to close his doors of sin.

She sent subliminal messages,
That joked about her pain
Laughed away the more challenging days
Accepting that love is to give,
And not to gain.

She screamed her answer loudest,
Experiencing her first broken heart
Cancer killing the one man,
Who softened her hardened heart.

Quiet Canvas

When I look at you,
I can't help but wonder
The many parts of me you've seen
I've been exposed to you
For my entire life
In my purest of forms
And darkest of means.

I am open to you,
Like a flower in a field
Blowing gently in the winds
Outside of you,
Wandering eyes see purity,
But you keep in my sins.

You hold the hidden truths
The ones I've buried and torn to pieces
Even the truth,
Of me lying in bed,
Praying that all of life ceases.

More than one of you exists,
All-seeing me
Throughout my years of life
One showing they know me better,
Another that they know me best
Amongst you all

I've caused great strife.

One would tell a story,
Of times I always smiled
And freely danced with grace
One would show a picture
Of the wrinkled smile
On my father's face.

Others would show times
I chose to be cruel,
And a mastermind of deceit
Still, another would show
Me trading in truths,
For moments I wanted to cheat.

I need to know,
Do you consider me crazy?
Or see me as sane?
You know me well,
Can you see the beauty
In my pain?

I've damaged some of you
Stripped you of the color,
Someone meant for you to be
Painted you with broken pieces of my past,
My present and future sinful sprees.

Blank Canvas

You are a masterful artist
Painting on walls blank and new
With strokes of lives lived,
You color bedroom walls
That only shows an incomplete you.

Think of all the places you've been,
The halls you've walked through
Would you even have a clue?
Can you imagine the impressions of you?
Collect all of your paintings,
Collage them together,
Would begin to project the
many stories of you.

These walls that hold
You darkest of sins,
Wrapped up in a cocoon
Will not allow you
To hide from your creation.
Try to wash off the paint,
Only to live long enough
to see yourself prune.

Prima Ballerina

The theatre grows quiet as the
music begins to fade in
Lively conversations cease
to respect her presence
There she stands, alone behind the curtain
Wanting it no other way
The next two minutes are hers to own.

She will be the center of all who stare in awe
The one who will create
emotions through movements
That some have never felt or seen.
She will be the creator of
an unforgettable performance,
The beauty that many will
continue to whisper about
For weeks after this day is done.

The high she is on,
Overwhelms every inch of her soul
She is primed, prepped, and ready
She stands there glistening in
her warm-up sweat.

She goes through the entire performance
Once more in her head
Perfecting every move

She will soon be making.
The music grows louder,
Her heart thumps with the melody
She counts down in her head
To the last few seconds before it's her cue.

Her head rises to try and catch the spotlight.
But it fades,
And the whispers begin to swirl again
The volume of voices rises once more
The music comes to a stop,
And her curtain never opens.

She races to rip them apart
But comes to find
There is no break in the sea of red.

She begins to scream
To catch the attention of someone,
Anyone who can help fix this madness
But finds herself awakened by her voice.

All she manages to say,
Is a soft "no"
This nightmare came again,
To remind her of the dream
She passed up many years ago.

Reverie

With widened eyes,
My mind drifts to a place of peace and rest
In my state of serenity,
I begin to envision a life
That will have its end,
Once reality catches up with my dreams.

I am free here
Relieved from life's sorrows,
And distant from Satan's touch
In this world,
There's an endless green pasture,
Flowers bloom for an eternity,
And birds fly through clear skies freely.

Then I see you
Skin that glistens,
And a smile that's untouched
by the grips of pain
Your eyes twinkle with a child's joy.
In our haven,
Death does not lay on the lips
Where your life was once choked out.

Pretty Storm

For us, love struck twice.
Its arrows pierced our hearts
At a time when life's true light
Was shielded from us
With the backs of our parents.
When our eyes had seen little evil
And our hearts remained foreign to pain.

If we could journey back
To that moment in time,
We would tell ourselves
To not be so quick
To rip that arrow out.

The second strike,
So much time had gone by
You went to live your life,
As I did mine.
But when our eyes met,
They did not shine
The way they had before
What stood in front of you,
Were millions of closed doors.

Please, steer clear
I was summoned by a storm
That looked like a dream
My time in captivity,
The storm became me
It's too late for us.
We're five years past
The days of purity.

But from your lips
You said with sureness,
"I love you."
I'm immovable by your words
For once upon a time
A storm whispered the same tale.

I must tell you my truth
Who you are loving
Is a portrait I drew
Making it to be
What I want everyone to see
But far from being me.

My eyes danced around
The word "why?"
You leaped in response saying,
"I love you
For who you are today
And I see the woman
You'll grow to be tomorrow."

I hope you are prepared
To show the words you speak
For A Pretty Storm is heading your way,
And I am no longer weak.

A Silver Platter and A Golden Spoon

Look at you.
Wishing for the stars
And hoping for a dream
With your eyes closed
And a faith that sees its end.

You drank from cups,
Others would see lined with gold.
You were fed the fat
From the healthiest cow.
Yet you remain still on your mother's breast.

You've grown complacent
Accepted being content
With what someone else
Has earned and allowed you to have.
Gone is the girl
With a beast inside the belly of a sheep.

Life showed its true colors, And broke you
But only with the permission
You allowed it to have
Its shackles are now bound to your calves.

You weren't ready for life,
But it was prepared for you
You're equipped with the tools
To bring life down to its knees
And ask YOU, what's next?

You have a purpose to fulfill
One that God spoke words,
Saying, "my child, you are marked."
The power to turn hateful hearts
The blood of royalty flows through you.

The enemy loves this place
In which you've found your comfort
Sit back and relax
Have a toast to celebrate
Greedy hands now caress your fate.

But go on
Keep laying there
Let the starving beast
Pass you by
You were never that hungry anyway.

Clear Skies

The One Who Keeps Knocking

I stopped listening to
You in my reality,
So, You began to speak
to me in my dreams

I Am Peter

It was easy for me to love You,
In my season of innocence and youth
Your name fell on the lips of children,
And fools who spoke the truth.

You placed me on my boat,
I set sail from the shores of You
But Your eyes were always on me,
While my focus became the oceans' blue.

I began to grow at peace,
With the known dimensions of my boat
I was the captain of my sail,
The only one keeping the crew afloat.

Too blind in pride to notice,
The glacier I was steering myself into
So You sent a storm my way,
In hopes of turning me back to You.

At first glance You were a blur
My mind was troubled in
believing if it was real
So I called out,
"If it is You, then help me to heal."

I was expecting a thunderous voice,
Or a dream like Joseph had
To my surprise You placed in my hands,
A pen and a writing pad.

"If this is really for me,
Then come and speak to me Yourself."
"Come." You said and I left my boat,
Then I began my journey back to health.

As I walked to You,
I wrote like I was running out of time
I created poems that the
world had never heard,
Because what You made for me is mine.

But then the winds filled with whispers,
From the crew I left behind
"How can your purpose be to write,
When there are others with greater minds?"

A chill ran down my spine,
As the cold waters began to rise
"Lord, save me!" and You did
From the doubting place where faith dies.

"You Can't Have The Soul You Never Created"

Our journey together must come to an end
I can no longer walk with someone
Who wears a mask to be my friend.

I lost pieces of me for your gain
I shouldn't have trusted you,
Who profits off my pain.

You fell hard for your pride
From leading Heavens worship,
To Hell's tour guide.

He paid the bill I racked up with you
So get my name outcho' mouth,
Now we are through.

Slave and master now separated
"You can't have the soul you never created."

Naked Love

Our eyes longed for one another
But our spirits couldn't touch,
And our hearts couldn't beat
To the same rhythm.

We were covered with the clothes
We layered on
Over our years of separate life
Intimacy was limited,
To love at first sight.

We covered our scars
And threw scarfs over our pain
Tight lips kept in our heartbreaks
We hid our stories
By placing jackets over our t-shirts
Never talked about
The shoes we had to walk in.

For a long time,
We forced one another
To function fully dressed
Causing friction between our fabrics,
And a knot of yarn
Developing in the center
Unknowingly, making each other
Pick new pieces

Of clothing to put on.

Our spirits yearned to be one
Ripping through matted fabrics,
And finding holes in places
Where yarn had grown thin.

Our hearts called to one another
Listening out for muffled beats,
And wanting to succumb
To the love it knew
We needed to give and receive.
So, the undressing began.

We took turns
Placing our hands on delicate places
Gently removed fabrics
Intertwined with our skin
We used our lips
To kiss the areas that needed love,
And salivate places

That had become dry.

Our eyes then saw
One another's weaknesses,
Insecurities and vulnerabilities
Our spirits leaped
Into an embrace of acceptance
Our hearts began
To beat in unison.

Then we stepped back to admire
The journey we ventured through
Allowed our eyes to finally see
The temple that God
Created for us to cherish.

In that moment,
We knew we had found
Our Naked Love.

White Flag

I am tired
The seed of anger I watered,
And rays of sin
I allowed to nurture it,
Has grown to be vines
Around my joy.

Who am I?
What have I become?
My actions were filled with rage
That I know cannot be undone.

I cry to You
Weeping on sinners' knees,
And clutching Your Word to my chest
I am ready
To walk with You again.

God, please forgive me.

I Am Pretty Bird

A bird's beauty is not defined
By the colored wings its
viewers stand in awe of
For what they see,
Is the starting frame of the bird,
And it's unknown journey ahead,
Or the conclusion from
the storm it weathered.

I am Pretty Bird.
My outer feathers are the gateway to my inner story
I hand to you the keys
By singing songs of poetry
That lure in hearts of curiosity
Allow my sacred songs to flow through
But be careful not to let your eyes be fooled
By my outer red to my inner blue
I allude confidence, balance, a known gift,
And shared love. That's true
Before you call me on my beauty,
I must share with you my pain.

I flew through a storm
Where the rain bruised
the feathers around my neck
Thunder raged louder than my thoughts,
Stifling my songs for help

Strikes of lightning blinded my path,
And winds ripped me off course
My wings became heavy
from soaking in the storm's cries
I fell from the sky's grace
As memories of loved ones passed me by
Gravity had its hands
on my plummet to reality
Other hands selfishly took from me
When "no" was uttered clearly
I was too weak to remind
myself of God's created beauty
I opened my beak to the intoxicating waters
Pouring from the clouds
As I prepared myself for the end,
God stretched out His hand towards me
My rebirthing began.

I am Pretty Bird.
My outer feathers
Tell the story of my inner beauty
I allude strength, renewal,
and a new beginning
God cleared my skies
And gave me new wings
Placed back in me a louder voice to sing
There is beauty in my pain
I have lived through loss
And loved through gain

But this cycle of life,
From clear skies to stormy weather,
Will continue for an eternity
I burn bright with the life breathed into me
I am equipped with fire to shed light
And a large wingspan to fight
You too are Pretty Bird.
Take your flight.

Acknowledgments

First and foremost, I give all glory, credit, appreciation, love, and gratitude to God. This book was built upon the faith, creativity, and gift He instilled in me. The process of starting this book was a tough one. The vision of completing it was difficult to maintain some days. But, along the way, He continued to provide me with the words to write my story. I hope that He is represented well throughout my words. I am human. I consider a part of my life a fall from His grace. But His love and protection never left me. Because of God, you are able to read my journey through pain and the transformation of it becoming my beauty.

To my father, it was because of his life's (taught) beauty that strengthened me to fight through my pain. It saddens me to have to write about him in the past tense. However, because he utilized and managed all of God's blessings so well over the time he had on Earth, I know he's being rewarded for eternity for being a great dad. He is the main inspiration to the entire first part of this book. His passing was the sole reason I picked up my pencil and began to write. His funeral was the first moment I recited my first ever poem and fell in love with the process. I wanted the world to know how grave a loss it was the day God called David Wayne Lewis home. Thank you, daddy, for helping me understand my purpose in life. You are such an impactful man that even in death, you still found a way to touch my heart and help me grow.

I would not have been able to complete this book without my mother. Aside from financially aiding in the editing and publishing process, she also supported my dream. Having graduated with no job, she gave me the continued space to thrive and write. Even in times when she didn't know fully the purpose I was pursuing, she always extended her patience, a listening ear, her wisdom, and her prayers. I am forever grateful for the grace she extended towards me when I needed her to. She is the ideal woman that I want to grow into someday for my children. Thank you, Doctor Anita Lewis.

Where do I even start in thanking the man who was the needed heartbeat to my writing? My fiancé, and husband to be, Donovan Johnson, thank you. He never gave up on me on days when I gave up on myself. When I thought that I couldn't possibly write another word, he gave endless encouragement. He would pause on any and everything when I needed to read a poem to him. He held me when I cried writing the poems that reminded me of painful times. He is my go-to, my biggest supporter, the inspiration to our Naked Love. The man who's never brought me pain and has always presented me with life's beauty. Thank you, my beautiful blessing, for being the man God created you to be for me.

To my older brother David Akim Lewis. You have a heart of gold that you selflessly share with those in your life. You extended its grace towards me, and I am thankful. You financially assisted me in ways to bring my dream to a reality.

We goofed many nights about me following this path. But, when it came down to it, you showed up for me when I needed it most.

To my youngest brother, Daniel Ali Lewis. Thank you for the moral support you extended towards me. Your positivity was very refreshing during my journey.

A special thanks to the God-fearing women in my life, Catherine Necco, Gabrielle Nobles, Bailey Clayton, Myra Cardenas, Kierra Bygrave, Georgia Lamb, and Jessica Ikoya. Thank you all for being the group of friends who held me accountable, checked in on me, prayed for me, and rooted for me. The women who I know would fight to be first in line to buy my books. The women who would go to battle with me. The women God placed in my life to lift me in prayers and love.

To everyone at Johnson Tribe Publishing, thank you. The courses, classes, experts, and support groups you presented me with assisted me in my writing journey, equipped me with the knowledge I needed to grow and better myself, and gave me my starting platform to break into the publishing world.

Finally, thank you to Ms. Latanga Spencer, my 8th-grade teacher and much- needed mentor. The expertise, wisdom, time, and energy you extended towards me throughout my writing process was invaluable.

About The Author

Dominique Alya Lewis is the creative genius behind the phenomenon, Alya Skye. After graduating from Houston Baptist University with a degree in marketing, she wanted to follow her life's calling by entering into the world of writing. She gained inspiration from her childhood creative outlets such as dance, theatre, and band. Falling in love with the works of Lauryn Hill and the late great Maya Angelou inspired her, even more, to create stories from her love of words. Before releasing her first book, (My) Pain is Beauty, Dominique shared her passion on multiple social media platforms under her alias Alya Skye, where she released poems, original quotes, inspirational pieces of her writing, and more. Now being a published author, she hopes to continue on this path of creativity and has her sights set on greater career goals as an author, writer, and poet. To continue following Alya Skye on her journey, follow her on Instagram, Twitter, YouTube channel, and Facebook @Authoralyaskye and her website **http://alyaskye.com** for more of her work.